THANKSGIVING

A TRUE BOOK

by

Dana Meachen Rau

Children's Press®

A Division of Grolier Publishing

New York London Hong Kong Sydney
Danbury, Connecticut

The Macy's Thanksgiving Day Parade

Reading Consultant
Linda Cornwell
*Coordinator of School Quality
and Professional Improvement
Indiana State Teachers
Association*

Author's Dedication
*For Aunt Joanne
and Uncle Jon*

**Visit Children's Press® on the
Internet at:
http://publishing.grolier.com**

Library of Congress Cataloging-in-Publication Data

Rau, Dana Meachen, 1971-
    Thanksgiving / by Dana Meachen Rau.
        p.   cm. — (A true book)
    Includes index. 5-21-07
    Summary: Describes the history, customs, meaning, and celebration of Thanksgiving
        ISBN 0-516-21515-9 (lib. bdg.)   0-516-27063-X (pbk.)
    1. Thanksgiving Day—Juvenile literature. 2. United States—Social life and customs—Juvenile literature. [1. Thanksgiving Day. 2. Holidays.]
I. Title. II. Series.

GT4975.R38 2000
394.2649—dc21   99-085973

Contents

On Thanksgiving, families are thankful for being together to share a special meal.

Giving Thanks

Look at the word "Thanksgiving." If you switch the word around it says, "giving thanks." Thanksgiving is a holiday in November. It is a time for people to think about the things they are thankful for.

Harvest festivals have been an important part of world history for thousands of years. On these

days, people gathered for a large feast after they harvested a good crop. People also set aside days to thank God for their blessings or for helping them through hard times. The first Thanksgiving drew on these traditions.

The Pilgrims

The Pilgrims lived in England. But they could not worship God there the way they wanted. So they decided to start a colony of their own in America.

In 1620, the Pilgrims set sail on a ship called the *Mayflower*. One hundred and two people, including thirty children, made

The Pilgrims leave England for a new land.

the long journey and landed in Plymouth, Massachusetts, on December 11, 1620. The Pilgrims were not prepared for the rough winter ahead. They had no homes, and food was running low. About half of the Pilgrims died that winter.

Lack of food and shelter made the first winter a deadly season for the Pilgrims.

Plymouth Rock

In Plymouth, Massachusetts, people come from far away to see a large granite boulder that sits in a pit on the shore.

Some people believe that this rock is the one the Pilgrims first stepped on after their voyage. It is a special symbol of hope for success in a new land.

A monument has been erected to protect the rock from rough weather— and people.

A helpful Indian befriended the Pilgrims.

Finally, spring arrived. The Pilgrims met the Wampanoag Indians who lived in the area. The Native Americans welcomed the Pilgrims and taught them how to survive. They taught

The Indians taught the Pilgrims where to hunt and fish.

them how to plant corn, pump-
kins, and squash, and showed
them the best places to hunt
and fish. Thanks to the Indians'
help, the Pilgrims harvested a
good crop in the fall of 1621.

The Feast

The governor of Plymouth
Colony, William Bradford, wanted to have a large feast for the
Pilgrims to celebrate the good
harvest and to thank God for
their survival. The celebration
lasted for three days. Pilgrim
men hunted for wild ducks,
geese, and possibly turkey.

After the hunt, men brought turkeys and other game to be prepared for the feast (left). A treaty between Massasoit and the Pilgrims brought peace (below).

14

(The Pilgrims often used the word "turkey" to refer to any kind of wild bird.) Massasoit (MASS-uh-soyt), chief of the Wampanoag Indians, and ninety of his braves brought five deer for the meal.

The Pilgrims collected fish, lobsters, oysters, and clams from the shore. There were carrots, beans, onions, berries, and dried fruit. The Pilgrims probably didn't eat pumpkin pie because they had used up most of their flour. But they probably had boiled pumpkin and corn bread.

Cooking such a meal was a large task. The five women of the colony cooked everything over outdoor open fires. With

A woman in costume prepares a Pilgrim-style feast for visitors to a historical park.

The First Thanksgiving

so many people, the food was served outside on long wooden tables. Some guests may have sat on the ground.

The feast probably took place in mid-October. It was not only a time for eating, but

Men displayed their shooting skills at the feast.

also a time for prayer, singing, and games. There were races and wrestling matches. The men showed off their skills shooting guns and bows and arrows.

Thanksgiving Celebrations

The feast at Plymouth in 1621 is often called The First Thanksgiving. But Thanksgiving was not celebrated every year after that. The harvest in 1622 was not successful, so the Pilgrims did not celebrate. In 1623, a long rain saved the crops, and Governor Bradford

declared November 29 a day of thanks. Some people call this day, not the feast of two years earlier, The First Thanksgiving.

More colonies were settled
in America, and each named
days of thanksgiving when they
wanted to. There might be no
Thanksgiving one year, and

A colonial Thanksgiving,
recreated at a historical
site in Massachusetts

A group of Pilgrims make their way to church.

then two the next year. People celebrated by gathering in the town meetinghouse, praying to God, and then eating a large meal at home.

Thanksgiving was mostly celebrated in Massachusetts and the other New England colonies where people from Massachusetts had settled. By the late 1600s, people in Massachusetts chose November 25 as their yearly day of thanks. People in other colonies chose their own dates. Some didn't celebrate Thanksgiving at all.

In October 1777, the first American government, called the Continental Congress, declared

The Battle of Saratoga (above); President George Washington (1732–1799) (left)

the first national Thanksgiving, which meant that all thirteen colonies celebrated it. The colonists were fighting against England for their freedom in the Revolutionary War (1775–83) at the time. They were thankful for winning an important battle in Saratoga, New York. The Continental Congress pro-claimed yearly Thanksgiving days until 1783.

Five years later, President George Washington proclaimed

a Thanksgiving day on November 26, 1789. Washington wanted to celebrate the freedom and success of the new United States after the war. The Thanksgiving Proclamation was the first presidential proclamation in the United States.

Thanksgiving was still not a yearly event. Washington declared another one in 1795, and President James Madison declared two in 1815. After

President
James Madison
(1751–1836)

this, it was left to individual
governors in each state to set
their own Thanksgivings. By
1860, Thanksgiving was celebrated in all but two states.

A National Holiday

A writer and editor named Sarah J. Hale thought that all the states should celebrate Thanksgiving on the same day every year. For more than twenty years, she wrote articles and letters urging the presidents to make Thanksgiving a national holiday. The Northern

Sarah Josepha Hale
(1788–1879)

states were fighting with the
Southern states in the American
Civil War (1861–65). Hale thought
that a national Thanksgiving
would help bring the country
back together.

President
Abraham Lincoln
(1809–1865)

President Abraham Lincoln agreed. In 1863, he proclaimed the last Thursday in November as Thanksgiving Day—a yearly holiday for the entire nation.

Americans celebrated Thanksgiving on the last Thursday in November until 1939. In 1939, President Franklin D. Roosevelt changed the date to the third Thursday so there would be more time between Thanksgiving and Christmas. Most people disagreed with him. In 1941, Thanksgiving became the fourth Thursday in November and has been ever since.

Thanksgiving Today

Today, families and friends come together to celebrate Thanksgiving. Most people gather around a large table for a feast. In the center of the table may be a cornucopia (kor-new-KO-pee-a), a cone-shaped basket that holds grapes, nuts, and other fruit.

The horn-shaped basket we know today as the cornucopia was made from an animal horn in ancient times.

The word "cornucopia" means "horn of plenty."

A Thanksgiving

Corn is a common symbol of Thanksgiving. People hang ears of corn on their doorways or lay it on the table as a centerpiece. Before coming to America, the Pilgrims had never seen corn. The Indians showed them a special way to plant it. They heaped dirt into little hills. Then they planted three or four kernels of corn and some fish into each hill. The fish was food for the corn to help it grow.

Symbol

Bringing in the corn harvest

The Pilgrims had many uses for corn. They often dried it to make corn meal, which they used for corn bread and corn mush.

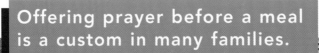
Offering prayer before a meal is a custom in many families.

Before sitting down to dinner, people often pause to give thanks for all of the blessings they have received during the year. Most families eat turkey as their main dish. They may also eat gravy, stuffing, cranberry sauce, vegetables, sweet potatoes, and rolls. Pumpkin pie is a popular dessert. After eating such a large dinner, many people often joke that they feel as "stuffed" as the turkey!

Parades have become a popular Thanksgiving tradition. For more than seventy years, the Macy's Thanksgiving Day Parade has marched through the streets of New York City. Two million people pack the sidewalks to watch the bands, floats, and large balloons pass by. A lot of other people watch the Macy's parade, or one of the other major parades, on television.

Macy's Thanksgiving Day Parade brightens New York City streets each year.

Football is a popular activity for many on "Turkey Day."

Sports are also a part of the holiday, just as they were at the first Thanksgiving. Fall is football season, so some people play football in their backyards. Others relax indoors and watch football on television.

Thanksgiving is also a time to help others. People often

These volunteers are serving poor and homeless people a turkey dinner with all the trimmings.

volunteer at local shelters to serve meals to the hungry.

No matter how Thanksgiving is celebrated, it is a time for families to feast together and think about all of the reasons they have to give thanks.

Some families may spend part of the Thanksgiving holiday in church.

To Find Out More

Here are more places to learn about Thanksgiving and other holidays:

 Books

Child, Lydia Maria. **Over the River and Through the Wood.** North South Books, 1998.

Corwin, Judith Hoffman. **Thanksgiving Crafts.** Franklin Watts, 1995.

Doherty, Katherine M. and Craig A. Doherty. **The Wampanoag.** Franklin Watts, 1995.

George, Jean Craighead. **The First Thanksgiving.** Paper Star, 1996.

Hintz, Martin and Kate Hintz. **Thanksgiving: Why We Celebrate It the Way We Do.** Capstone Press, 1996.

Miller, Marilyn. **Thanksgiving.** Raintree/Steck-Vaughn, 1998.

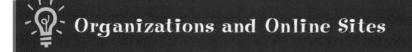

Organizations and Online Sites

Festivals.com
RSL Interactive
1001 Alaskan Way
Pier 55, Suite 288
Seattle, WA 98101
http://www.festivals.com/

Visit this site to find out about all types of festivals, holidays, and fairs around the world.

The Holiday Page
http://wilstar.com/holidays

Find out about your favorite celebrations at this web site, which is devoted to holidays.

Plimoth Plantation
P. O. Box 1620
Plymouth, MA 02362
http://www.plimoth.org

Learn all about the Pilgrims, the First Thanksgiving, and how to visit this historical museum in Massachusetts.

Important Words

colony a territory that has been settled by people from another country and is controlled by that country

crop a plant grown in large amounts, usually for food

harvest festival a celebration to give thanks for a good crop

meetinghouse a building where people of a town meet together

national to do with, belonging to, or characteristic of a whole country

proclaim to make public and official

symbol an object that stands for something else

tradition a custom, idea, or belief that is handed down from one generation to the next

Index

Meet the Author

Ever since Dana Meachen Rau can remember, she has loved to write. A graduate of Trinity College in Hartford, Connecticut, Dana works as a children's book editor and has authored many books for children, including biographies, nonfiction, early readers, and historical fiction. She has also won awards for her short stories.

When Dana is not writing, she is doing her favorite things—watching movies, eating chocolate, and drawing pictures—with her husband Chris and son Charlie in Farmington, Connecticut.